The Sandwich Man

The Sandwich Man

by
Donald J. Norman-Cox

ISBN-13: 978-0692442326

Arising Together Publishing

Printed in the United States of America

For dreams who've lost their dreamers
and dreamers who've lost their dreams.

Foreword
by Dr. Deborah Needleman Armintor

Unabashedly musical, the book that you are holding in your hands demands not only to be read but also to be heard. The best way to take it in, I believe, is to read it aloud. Don't worry that you might be caught talking to yourself, for you are never alone in a book like this: full as it is of calls and responses, jokes between reader and author, riffs, refrains, and a vibrant cast of characters interacting with each other and with you, encountering mysteries and problems that you're all trying to figure out together. Read it aloud, and you will find yourself singing it rather than speaking it, and swaying your body and stomping your foot. The stanzas come alive with sound and syncopation, and each description is lyrically and conceptually new and delightful: "pipe smoking" becomes a "souvenir of optimism," and bags packed for a journey are "crammed with past participles" (and that's just what first caught my eye when I opened the book at random just now to dig for examples. As it turns out, the book is so full of examples like these that I didn't have to dig at all). The Sandwich Man is of course written in words, not in musical notation, but it will ring in your ears like a bebop jazz record, full of riffs, jokes, refrains, and improvisations on themes, familiar, semi-familiar, and unknown. You are not just a reader, you are part of the band. And that makes sense, since The Sandwich Man originated as the product of an interactive collaboration between audience and author.

Its author, Donald J. Norman-Cox, once described The Sandwich Man to me as a puzzle. All good poetry is a kind of puzzle, I believe–a sequence of pieces, put together by artist and reader. The Sandwich Man is an especially unusual kind of poem-puzzle in that a number of its pieces were created by audience members at one of Donald's recitals at the University of North Texas (UNT). Audience members scribbled words on scraps of paper, blank puzzle pieces, and Donald cobbled them together into a narrative poem, full of music, lyrical prose, rich dialogue, sadness, laughter, and mystery.   And it's up to you, the lucky reader, to make it come alive. Call it a puzzle or a sandwich, but it's yours to make and enjoy. The ingredients Donald has provided you with are top-notch, and you will relish whatever it is you end up making of them.

I first met Donald when I was a member of UNT's Ghanaian percussion and dance group, led by the incomparable Professor and Master Drummer, Gideon Alorwoyie. I was by far the oldest and least skilled member of the ensemble, but having been their fan ever since I moved to Denton, Texas, and started teaching in UNT's English Department, it was for me the most sublime joy imaginable to participate in something so exquisite. The drumming and the dancing literally took my breath away, for it was not only emotionally moving, but physically challenging as well. Donald was a fan of the group too, and had asked Professor Alorwoyie and his group to help him bring to life one of his first literary compositions, the playfully titled "Dances of Saints and Heathens," one of several prior incarnations of the book you now hold in your hands. As I got to know Donald in this context, and came to experience the complex, open, and improvisational way his mind worked, I quickly came to realize that he is a rare kind of artistic genius. An intuitively musically-minded writer, he has that rare artistic ability to make familiar words, sights, smells, and sounds new and mysterious again, to make ordinary signifiers leap off the page and sing at us with music and meaning. He is, like one of this book's principle characters, an artist who took years to discover the unique masterpiece he was meant to create.

Deborah Needleman Armintor
Denton, Texas

From the Author

The Sandwich Man originated as a puzzle, it's pieces being a collection of responses to the questions: what is around the corner and what is over the track. A complete list of the responses is available on the book's website.

Often while assembling the puzzle, the work was asked "what are you about?" Answers were cryptic.

Typically, challenges of a difficult puzzle diminish as pieces are assembled. Yet, each time this work appeared to approach completion, the big picture remained elusive. Complicating the dilemma, the overall work did not conform to any literary convention known by this author.

Ironically, embracing the poem's desire for secrecy revealed its story line. Thereafter, literary devises were liberally inserted to obstruct a reader's comprehension and detour logic into places of uncertainty. Each obstacle increased the poem's authenticity, latitude, strength and fidelity to itself.

Obviously, decryption is necessary for proper comprehension, but merely persevering through the muddle is unlikely to produce an accurate decoding. Rather, the better tips for deciphering this work are: 1) read slowly, and 2) ignore context clues.

Finally, while the storyline is intentionally blurry, the poem's structure is not part of the riddle. The following chart is offered to reduce confusion.

The alphabets below represent indenture settings.

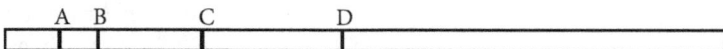

```
    A  B      C          D
 ┌──┬──┬──────┬──────────┬──────────────────┐
 └──┴──┴──────┴──────────┴──────────────────┘
```

1. Italic text beginning at D are Sandwich Man's spoken words.
2. Italic text beginning at C are Sandwich Man's thoughts.
3. Italic text beginning at A or B are statements by someone other than Sandwich Man.

www.arisingtogether.com/sandwichman.html

1.
They

The Sandwich Man

They,
from hearsay,
learned A and countless hues.

Others they'd learn soon enough,
    maybe.

But this,
hearing so much about it
    over,
    over,
    and over,
    again and
    ... and ...
    again,
like innocence
    – never privy to secrets –
they wanted passionately,
hoped
    – no –
needed
to know for themselves.

Come
  "a ma'velous day, yet golden,"
as Miss. Ma'am prophesied before each
  "...gotta get to them bells, Honey" –
            "Yeah. Sapphire ev'ry Tuesday. Fridays Pearl."
                      "Not Wednesdays?"
        "Never Sundays."
                  "Glitter every Thursday?"
    "... and Mondays."
                "Mm-hmm" –
an eggshell form with livid eyes watched grizzly grating hands
unshackle protective hugs;
moors to their sleeping she-warden: Miss. Ma'am's lieutenant.
  Raspy.
  Squatty.
  Simple.
  Pregnant.

All the time she laughed,
  "Miss. Ma'am, you so sassified."
  "Miss. Ma'am, you so skanky."
  "Miss. Ma'am, you so ..."
      "...sanctified?"

Gold plated crooked teeth smiled nervously,
  "Yeah,"
hiding a belly swelling cautiously,
  but proud,
  elated,
  hopeful.

  "Hmph. Whatever ain't never, 'cause whosoever,"
Miss Ma'am parried back
  cryptically,
  defiantly,
  thankfully,
  often.
She too, anxiously on guard.

Strip-quilted cape in tow, they
    – minuscule escapees ignoring sudden prayers,
    raspy screams,
    bludgeoning –
began their favorite leisure,
brushing cautiously passed piles of dozing rabbits
              "*Hares.*"
or hares impeding flocks of fun-loving roosters,
    – straw with wheat trim,
    hand stitched crookedly; and
inching off fatigued mattresses heavily stained,
    – wine with blood and asparagus;
glossing around fading Lilies,
    Daisys,
    Roses tempting desperate asters,
    larkspurs,
    snapdragons sequestered in claustrophobic coffee bins with
corners unfinished.

Deafening screams continuing; a second voice shrieking.

Into unlit halls the pack maneuvered
down countless treacherous stares;
passed a closet for murdered bones,
    mud-caked shovels; and ...
behind a jade loveseat and crippled lounger
    – old, frayed, argentine;
under a wobbly table for cards,
    boisterous,
    cigar smoking,
    all wearing monochrome shoes perilously near a pompous new
RCA Victor console reporting weather in living color.

Horrific shrieks continued.
A third voice baying and baying, and ...
    "*I see ya and I double ya. I double ya,*"
young ears heard a whinny voice vow.

They
    – building strength –
raced back and forth,
    back and forth,
    accelerating senselessly,
    smearing all plausible pragmatism,
    halting at a hot pink leopard print door.

Still life was not their forte, yet.

Bursting into the kitchen
they built cornbeef sandwiches
    – oily, gooey –
larger than life.

One, avocado trimmed;
pink sherbet globs on another,
    and cornflakes,
    mustard,
    cotton candy,
    cinnamon.
Prohibited boysenberry on two for one.
Rainbow of sprinkles, chose another.

Dementedly, they
    – into halves perfectly unequal –
sawed them with a toy sword,
    – found, platinum, squared, useless;
                "Definitely not the sharpest?"
foil-encasing each still-moist half as does an uncle;
doubled for rain.

One scream;
    another;
    all screams stopped so suddenly.
No whimpers.
No noise.
Nothing.

Furiously, they crammed
hand-me-down galoshes,
    diapers,
    bubbles,
    candy apple, more, plus
a tiger with lion polka dots
    – accidentally ruining the tiger's eye –
and mutilated sandwiches
    into a hand painted lunch box; lunch box
    into a dinosaur backpack; backpack
    onto resolute shoulders, and
into a day so golden indeed, they
    – shushing disorderly rabbits or hares, plaid ones;
    disregarding an iridescent door's beacon –
climbed out the latest broken window,
    overjoyed,
    overconfident,
    overdressed in red's hefty courage,
    yellow's non-discrete gladness,
    green's ingenious and virtue;
    palettes tethered unstylishly to a camel hair shirt
    – reminder of something again forgotten.

So bold. So unique.
        "So chintzy. So schmaltzy"
        "So whosoever, she would'da said?"

Accompanied by Spring's avidity,
      "It should be easy to find,"
one figured, prompting,
      "So much she say about it?"

After each turn came another,
… another;
another and …
another.
And nothing either imagined.

Over desert-ish mountains they searched all morning.
    Prairies, noon and afternoon.
Mammoth oceans, the forests they searched
    – fruitless –
all day and evening.

Exactly when predicted,
    as always,
Madam Dusk and company
    gloriously bedazzled in temptation
came a-sauntering by;
    day's temporal apex when life is pointless without extra rounds
    of patty cake,
    hide and seek,
    kickball,
    tick-tag,
    played between themselves, only.
                "It should'da been easy to find?"
one worried, prompting,
          "So much her say about it. Liar."

Rumblings came,
    and bells,
    and birds,
    and stopped,
    then ran away.

Facing potential knights of danger,
one
    – supposedly boldest –
solicited,
          "Where is 'round the corner?"
to hungry ignorables comparing depleted souls;
worldly pundits replete with used sea tales,
    penniless,
    rumpled,
suggesting they'd been there awhile,
often.

One said,
>   "That's the street | 'round | from where | you live."
>   "But, I passed many streets?"

One said,
>   "Yeah, keep going. | Its five or ten minutes | away."
>   "In the future? But he said..."

One said,
>   "Just around | the river bend. Keep going. | Watch for outhouses."
>   "For outhouses? But..."

>   "Keep going!"
they commanded together.

The ignorables knew them well;
knew about them;
knew their uncles;
knew their mother
>   or claimed so, back when they had money.

Overpowered, pluckiness gloomed,
>   moped,
>   fretted,
>   scowled.

Scariness
>   – hiding, scrutinizing –
not knowing what else to do insisted they counter with,
>   "Who named the numbers."
>   "Yeah but..."

scratching,
itching,
>   ignoring punishments for crimes unremembered,
>   "Say it!"
>   "Who named the numbers!"

Soup line creeping,
>   stomachs aching,
>   loathing such innuendo;
stabbing cleverly through layers of dismissal

nonplussed men speculated freestyle
deviously theorizing of destiny,
direction,
inevitability
    – so skillfully, so deceptively –
viciously divulging nothing,
    violently,
    savagely,
    excessively.

Such rebuffing,
such pooh-poohing,
    so overwhelming,
they
    – wonder-bound playmates wondering how men get that way;
    unwrapping a smeared sandwich;
            "yuk";
    too uninspiring,
    too unexciting,
    discarding it –
left.

Nose seeking crescent moons;
eyes piercing darkness vigilantly, diligently;
    one alerted the others,
          *"We just got'ta walk 'round a corner to
          get our destination?"*
From reassurance
    – if only for company –
came,
        "Around the corner, though not seen, is near."

Traversing giant mosaics
    – abstract silhouettes like themselves,
    clearly invisible,
    simple but convoluted –
one heard clouds pass, willows grow.

Others heard
>hair pressing, clothes folding, A and B selections;
>dozen playing, chicken raising, blues, crap shooting;
>knife pulling, sirens, handcuffs, gunfire;
>laughing, switch-getting, cornbread making, fried.

Surrounded by confusion so impenetrable
>they way-fared,
>watched,
>wondered, and
>... wanted to know so passionately.

Around story time
>– moon strategically placed for
>suspense,
>thrills,
>adventure,
>goose bumps –
a nocturnal ballet broke out:
>feckless pageantry,
>curious odorants,
>jangles,
>reckless spectacle.

>*"So perfect enough?"*
a rose painted madam
>– cheap tobacco chewer,
>undervalued,
>overpriced –
would whisper prayerfully before heading blindly to the bells.
>*"Ruddy be rich,"*
and
>*"use soap; avoid the blues,"*
and
>*"greens be good for ya,"*
they misheard her tell.

Shadows whispered,
    "She so opalescent,"
and
    "florescent and iridescent"
                  "'Oh, what a time so promising', she
                  say."

Some said,
    "She so..."
        "...Looney?"
            "Maybe."

From revelers tending a jazzmaker's crime,
    "Killing it! He killing it!"
they heard and wanted to know.

But, this effort being a while too long,
    despite the commotion,
    wrapped in ambivalence,
    beneath a strip quilt guardian,
they...

slept.

*   *   *

2.
Something Happened

Constant ruckus,
itinerant fog,
wind chimes' bewitching incantations
   – simmering –
brewed wealth for discordant playmates abundantly rich with
muddle.

A non-deciphered dowry discreetly haunting some:
   "The sun be brightest wherever fate ain't";
           "...sometimes she say."
others hunting discretely another tasteful sandwich – they
spied extraordinary distractions:
   three peddlers,
   two grungy,
   one plump in sorcerer's garb: tie dyed scrubs and ghastly
   umbrella under skies so clear, so pacifist ...
        "So baffling.
        So ghoulish."
               "Magnates and moguls?"
     "Yes."
creeping giant appliances from a megalopolis kind of place
   so humongous.

"*So mysterious. So complex.*"
                    "*Pigment factory?*"
    "*Ye--yes.*"
Byzantine enterprise with horns;
boarded Gothic windows
    – diamond and pearl zebra striped;
dressed in olive jungles
        overrun with oaks,
        elms,
        willows.
Maze of messy molehills –– no moles.
                "*Laughters and sobs?*"
Laugh-shrouded sobs.

        "*Carrot stooped. Thistle fortressed.*"
            "*Mm-hmm.*"
        "*Big corn. Magic. 'Bout oowee-big with ...*"
            "*A and A.*"

They knew A.
The others, they'd learn later.
    Maybe.

Under the magic corn gold-plated teeth welcomed four puppies
    before their mother died from unwarranted thrashings,
    reprimands,
    pregnancy's penance.

Crude wool canopy read Miss. Ma'am's Emporium.

Gall and gaudiness spelled,
Decadence or excessive gloss baited
they
    – many times –
circled the bafflement,
    scooting, just ... scooting.
Everybody.
The whole way, in filthy diapers, scooting.

"So massive, so astounding,
so ..."

> *"Maybe, maybe... maybe ... maybe."*

Amid one tour, the alarming peddler in scrubs
    – larger, shorter –
saluted.
Others did nothing,
       "Tyros."

More to watch a flight of birds than hobnob or exhaustion,
everyone paused.
    And heard bells.
    And heard rumbling.
    And knew nothing.
        "Nothing."

Fearlessness
    – unmindful of being a sandwich short –
wondered boldly,

> *"How do we find 'round the corner?*
> *Where do worms play?*
> *Who named the numbers?"*

Cowardly,
cautiously,
allies and confidants
disapproving,
disappeared.

"Just a little ways more.
...no questions...
...go faster...
...be careful...
...less noise...
...turn left and we're there."

Uncertainty muffled,
       "What will we find!"

"Shhs!"
The tyros grumbled,
  "We?"

        "Where'd..."

Tyranny resting,
  "Success."

        "Success?"
"Tranquility."
        "Success with tranquility?!"
"At last, peace and comfort."
        "Lasting peace and comfort?!!"
*"Shhs. Y'all g'on in. Got women waiting to welcome you,
and you can stay all the day long."*

Disgruntled with nothing to barter,
  the tyros left.

Jubilant,
  ecstatic,
Happiness –
  visioning something good,
    thinking:
        "Oh, what a day so magnificent." –
autocratically,
most authoritatively
bestowed the brutish merchant
        "...the last half sandwich?"
warmish,
distorted, but
        "mature, dramatic, tasteful?"
with jalapeños and extra sprinkles.

Offer declined.

Plainly the least worked was overheard muttering,
  "Too hot under this cruel canopy or worse."

From inside, heedful ears heard in piercing timbre,
"I see ya hat, an' raise ya mo'.
Double ya.
Yeah. I'ma double ya."

Familiar.

In handmade coconut shoes proudly tied all by themselves,
the bravest
   – alone,
   lankier,
   sweating –
briskly turned left once,
   discovering again,
the fearsome tyrant
   colossal,
and tyro
   – one –
more grungy, now hatless.

                  "Is here it?"
twirling secretly a forgotten sword,
squared handle peeking from a cookie size hand.
Painfully, the tyro slave – unaided – jammed mammoth laundry
   tables through a new screen door, ripping it.
Huge idle overseer hissing,
   "No! Move! Too slow!
   Stop letting stuff distract ya. Lose the weight!"

Instantly,
a freeloading tiger and other baggage not pastel or light
escaped a dinosaur.

Much faster, a second left happened.
There again, the creature in scrubs
   – enormous –
squeezing sewing paraphernalia through quaint narrow doors,
   alone.

To each from the other,
  "You again?"

The creature, some called a beast
  – struggling to fathom the problem;
  patting him roughly with hands strong and grating –
paused to teach him I.
  "Wonder what's holding ya back?"

Avoiding eye contact, Remorse
  – panting, mortified –
atoned, whimpering,
          "Sir, we – I – got more sandwiches."
  "Oh no!"
the beast impugned,
  "There's fungus in ya cedar chest coffer, stuffed in a worthless
  backpack obviously crafted by someone blind. But! This
  impressive, bronze-washed bag great for toting important stuff
  like yours? It I'll trade for that worn, childish backpack and rust
  bound box. Pay me nothing more – I – like you."

Self-absorption,
  veiling angry spats between canopy and wind
  plotted,
          "What a great deal?"
                  "That's what smart guys got?"
          "We'll be great, cool, and stylish, stepping 'round the
          corner with our lunch in a bag? Such flattery."

"We? I. Say I."

                  "We – I – like flattery?
                  Miss Ma'am say we'll be … I'ma be
                  covered in flattery all our life?"

"Shhs -- quickly -- no questions."
                  "But if they don't like it…"
"They will."

                  "But if they don't?

"Trade it,"
replied the demon
raising his umbrella.

"Where?"

"A store."

"What store?"

"Any store."

"Where?"

"Around the corner."

"But, I don't..."

"Shhs."

A fourth left
    completed before his sentence
found the boldest where he and fickle friends started,
    – larger, lessor, sweltering –
mangling thoughtlessly a platinum sword
    fully concealed in roomier hands,
communing with kindred
    – a brothel –
disregarded,
irregular,
shunned by friends.

So familiar.

Achromatic-lesson learning:
    "Avoid the path devoid of rights."
    studied voices warned.

Drab bag holding:
    "Eyes without wisdom be blind."
    prudent voices remembered hearing.

True-blue friend losing:
    "It was you who abandoned us,"
    dimming voices chastised.

Doctored sign reading:
    ~~LaShi's Soup~~ Emporium –
        OUT OF BUSINESS
    ~~Aunt Shiya's Crafts~~ Emporium –
        OUT OF BUSINESS
    ~~Madam Shi's Palm Reading~~ Emporium –
        OUT OF BUSINESS
    ~~Shiya Mae's Laundry~~ Emporium –
        OUT OF BUSINESS

Twirling the hidden sword
    – rubbing it, mauling it –
the big corn with A-I-A-I
    – they knew A and I –
rolled away with worthless riches.
            "... Wait..."

Two shoeless uncles passed without living.
            "What?"

Sunshowers began,
    cloaking rumbles,
    seabirds,
    fading bells.

                    *   *   *

3.
Bologna

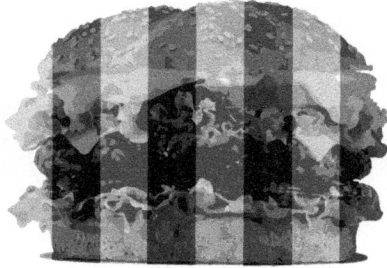

Left untended, havoc prospered. Anarchy conquered They.
Some grouched flamboyantly,
Others puked vulgarities
brazenly disrupting wave-making contests on a docile lake
    – formerly an ocean –
misdeeds cloaked by enharmonic lullabies heirloomed from
    dreamers
        ambition rich, fortune poor;
    one – their monarch – suspected of invading their keep.
        "Sure is."
                "Mm-hmm."

Her long abandoned sense forgotten.
    Anxiety overwhelmed reason.
    Reason overwhelmed optimism.
    Optimism once sang so sassified,
    "...A future ahead, somewhat unclear."
Still-lipped commoners echoed,
           "I wonder whatever I'm gonna find here..."

Miss Ma'am,
  – touring the empire –
preached prosperity
    to heathens,
    lowlifes,
    scoundrels –– patrons.

She
  – stopping to gamble once in a while –
won the house.
    Lost it.
Won it back.
    Lost it.
Winning it back,
    refused to play again.

Despising resilience,
    submission called her dumb,
    stupid,
    yet colored.
                    "Colored?"
          "Colored-colored or just colored?"
Both.

Fully armored, she continued,
    wholly holy.
Her final testimony to the realm:
    "Colors – treasures 'nuf for e'rybody, but who ya know ain't got
        none? Somebody.
    They's all good for something – donkey brown, eggplant, even
        fuzzy wuzzy. Funny ain't it? – even fuzzy wuzzy –
        and never lie, I say. See if they do.
    Be the clever change 'em, not the wise.
    Come together right, they strong. They stout. They be satisfying.
        They makes valya!
    Who do what, been where, when – they serves up that and a
        swallow for how come they done it. Hear 'em? Can ya?
    Listen with ya eyes. See 'em with ya ears. Taste 'em with chittlin's

and 'tatoe pie –– soul food make y'a see stuff different.
One be fancy. Another'n excites.
One be honeydew for hot summer nights.
But 'stead of pretty-picking and loving just that'n, need to see
them otherns, too – them that ain't easy. 'Cause only when they
stands together be when they's at perfection. What kinna pretty
can a garden be if the whole thing covered of inch worm?
E'ry one got valya. E'ry one gots weight. Na'on one need
na'on help keeping they business straight
'cause where they is be gumption, be guts, be pull, be sho'ness.
Where they ain't be confusion and hurt; rogues get rich, buncha
rats and rascals – got storm clouds raining turpentine for
murdering some; killing the otherns. And all the colorblind
sees nothing. Nothing.
But don't worry 'bout 'em. Forget 'em I say. 'Cause after e'ry
storm, here they all comes back and brings peace, and brings
grace, and says the sun still out there 'luminizing the road to
joy for whosoever. For whosoever I say! I say for who-so-ever!
Amen! And amen ...and... amen."

Raspberry pipe being her only riches,
rejection alone received her.

"Bimbo spaz think we can't see she blind."
"... Maybe."

Still, under skies cloudless and livid they
– unconsciously honoring her –
spite the world,
proudly flaunting before empty-handed others more opportuned,
a ghastly umbrella of pomp and power.   .
"A steal."
"A bargain?"
"It only cost a sandwich."
even as blood drops trickling their legs dried atop each other.

Without warning,
one beheld the Great Mo' W, noblest of countless

overdeveloped,
overpowering,
over-opinionated clones of linage much debated.
Everyone knows Great Mo' W,
fearlessly gowned in bronze and lava with orchids.
Most whisper in his presence.
The daring call him ruddy.

> *"Imperial Mo' W, The Magnificent*
> *know everything important."*

subservience whispered.

They,
nervously rising to padded knees,
bowing before the exalted ruler
– Mo' W's standard fee –
begged in unison,

> *"Where is 'round the corner,*
> *Your Excellence?"*

Another stolen bike dismounted,
"Look at 'ya.
Look at ya,"
his bullyship scowled with high pitched voice.

"Where did you go?"

> *"Oh. See, We..."*

"Hollow came
and you ran free,
friends and friends ran free."

> *"No, what had happened was..."*

"Now not full we feel."

> *"Beg pardon?"*

"Days full,
hollow,
days not hollow
where did you go?
Not we see,
as when you and friends and friends

ran free and free."

That optimistic day,
    so artful,
    crafty,
    discolored,
overcoming over-reliance on under-aged overlords,
they offered,

> *"o-O-oh. Thank you ...*
> *"Lake Rudolph."*
> *"Mm-hmm."*

* * *

4.
Song of the Goons

Before each day's only banquet everyone gathers in the place
　　– line starting at a ripped screen door –
waiting for groceries, bowled and bland.

Those arriving late, or
　　refusing to eat, or
　　too old, too slow, too ugly
　　or overeat,
sing:
　　"Dumb"
　　　　"Why they"
　　"shit"
　　　　"call me"
　　"Ass "
　　　　"My name"
　　"hole"
　　　　"is not."
　　"Sometimes I"
　　　　"answer 'em."
　　"Most times I"
　　　　"don't."

　　"Hit me"
　　　　"they"
　　"Laugh"
　　　　"sometime"
　　"Damn"
　　　　"I'm dumb"
　　"Fool"
　　　　"they say."
　　"Sometime I"
　　　　"make 'em nice.
　　"Most times I"
　　　　"won't."

　　　　　　　　　　　　　　　　　　The Sandwich Man

"*Outside I*"
    "*spit kick curse*"
"*Inside I*"
    "*cry, 'hello!'*
"*Crazy*"
    "*they*"
"*fool*"
    "*call me.*"
"*that's not*"
    "*my*"
"*name.*"

"*High*"
    "*I had*"
"*hopes*"
    "*but fate*"
"*Big*"
    "*ran my*"
"*dreams*"
    "*away*"
"*Sometimes I*"
    "*call them back*"
"*Most times I*"
    "*don't.*"

After feasting on slop, on a good day,
everyone gets a sandwich and says,
    "*mmm*"
From mmm, they learned M.
        "*A - I - M.*"
                "*A - I - A - I - M.*"

Maybe the rest they'd learn later.

* * *

5.
Chicken Salad

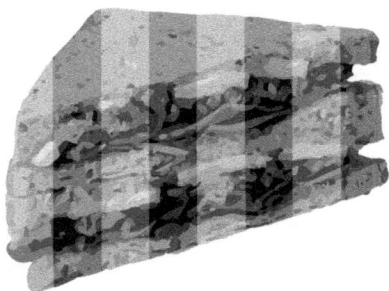

Nearly once,
precisely around the very-next-day-ish
    after commencing their search,
always thereafter,
    almost,
Miss. Ma'am mocked them.

She too,
    – diligently rummaging,
    hunting,
    pursuing –
searched,
begging the High and Almighty's guidance,
all along bragging,
    "I got a cross ta' track,"
joyfully,

incessantly,
laughing desperately,
    provoking
           "Ain't 'cross the track 'round the corner?"
                  "Hmm."

Masquerading in apathy, evasive eyes trailed her,
    endless minutes,
    endless hours,
chasing her through dreams and squalors,
    endless days,
    endless weeks,
convinced she'd expose perception's hiding place.

Then once,
    beyond endless months,
    countless years,
    increasingly sullen,
the impulsive one squandering summer's better days
    – plotting ambush, the high and mighty's, –
backed the wrong way,
shirtless,
scorching
    – sand to fallow;
    fallow to dirt;
    dirt to russet –
lewdly lauding a lullaby loudly,
incoherently,
    with fake tattoos;
mimicking the underhanded;
listening for guidance from the powerful,
    but inebriated;
lazy like their rumored father
    – conniving backslapping parasite never met –
learning treachery;
learning to ruse;
learning too, flattery's cost:

fairer the bag, higher the fare;
even for fawns and fawning.

Others,
    bashful,
    reluctant
    – also stalking the high and mighty –
heard only the song of goons.

Seeking salvation's scepter delivered Miss. Ma'am to insanity from where
    of all praises and scorns
she frequently waxed foolishly,
    "Whatever y'all say ain't got na'on sway,
    'cause whosoever gon' fly, one day."

Meanwhile,
rent overdue for a house she owned
cost unspeakable favors to grating hands,
    fists,
sometimes lamps,
    chairs,
    skillets;
fines for not turning enough tricks,
being blind,
    "putting the damn deed in a moron's name!"

Younger debtors of similar fees offered no respite,
goading,
                    "Why come answers wait for
                    questions?"
                    "Who named the numbers?"
persistently,
aggressively before evasively absconding.

Frustrated, had she caught them, welts would make.
Are pecking orders not horrific,
    until they change?

Once,
 amid resented mockery,
 before settling up for payless nights
entreaties for protection or weaponry
hollered,
 "The rod, the staff, they comforts me!"
As usual, rejection alone acknowledged her.

Pleading hysterically,
she searched hysterically,
 laughing,
greeting the inevitable hysterically,
 with sobs.

Meanwhile,
They, forever nonchalant,
 – repeatedly rubbing an indestructible sword –
selfishly plotted,
 "If she aint sharing, neither is we?"

Thereafter,
pacing familiar trails through elm infested oaks
 ceaseless,
 foreboding,
 cigarette littered – rummaging the remnants,
without her they persevered;
searching,
seeking,
 hunting rumbles, birds and bells,
listening too, for the high and mighty,
 and only the goons, they heard.

Stumbling over jagged rocks and phobias,
across crumbling isms and curbs,
into arrogance and ignominy's comforts;
 – fear's choice sustenance –
resistance surrendered,
overhearing tenor tones warn,

"*They'll kill yo' punk ass if I tell.
You can't do me. I ain't sced.*"

Then gravelly,
  "*Yeah? Keep talking.
  See what happen to ya,*"
rage replied.

Screams wanting to tattle,
    hid.
Childhood fading lashed,
          "*Cowards.*"

Misreading options,
repressing impulse,
gullibility feigning wisdom droned,
                "*Nawl. They always be making it hard
                for guys like me,*"
flashing cracked vocal tones with post-pubescent whine.
                "*Them others be bragging 'bout going
                there, being there, living there. But,
                I'm going? Hell yeah, I'm going. I ain't
                lying.*"

Constantly like neighboring voices,
discordant like jailhouse voices,
outcast like row house voices,
obscure like whorehouse voices,
faintly and fainter lashed one and a band of childish tempers,
          "*Cowards.*"
Cowards they swore,
    and vanished.

Well anyway, his new friends were better.
Adolescence
    – tall, willowy –
    seeking vigor for independence and self-confirmation
prepared half a sandwich,

deleting edges,
pinching off tiny bites.

Obliviousness
     – scruffy, fixated;
nipping,
nibbling,
gnawing,
assessing,
     offering anyone unlike himself none –
helped pinch annoying crust to extinction
     and
the rite of consumption began.

Tastebuds salivating,
     eyes closed hallucinating,
preparing for that delicious first full sight.
Stepping away,
     stalking satisfaction,
     awaiting gladness,
     eager to know its delight.
Dreaming, fantasizing,
     anticipating intimacy,
Fashioning, hoarding, ogling ecstasy;
awaiting that perfect moment when pleasure indescribable ...
     "You gonna have that?"
Someone pried.

Gazing angrily, unpolished machismo growled,
                    "What's it to ya?"
     *"Man, na'on one 'a y'all's so-called uncles tu'nt the corner 'cause
     they can't get 'cross them tracks. Neither will you."*

Soul wide open. Senses prepared for rapture,
Rashness
     – always available –
snickered absentmindedly.
                    "Hmm. Potential prey?"

Someone watched,
drooling a blissful feast;
    a prize,
    comforter,
most original,
    tasteful,
    gratifying.

Victory cleverly flanked unseen as imprudence enticed,
                "The track? You know where to cross."

Enraptured if not spellbound,
Someone jabbered,
    "Maybe."

Confident poker face slid toward pure delirium,
    provocatively,
    defiantly,
    tortuously,

              "Maybe?"
      "It's a secret. You gotta be ratified to know."

Irrationality
    – joining the mayhem –
repined,
    parting impatient teeth.

Someone's lips quivered,
    "But...um..."

              "Say where they creep 'cross the track,"
hypnotically,
trance inducing,

              *"Say where they wanders from here to
              there."*

Far past deprivation
    – lip licking,

courting desperation
   – heaving, gasping,
approaching obsession
   – hand rubbing,
Someone
   – swallowing nothing –
lip-licked again.

Borrowing contempt's insolent grin,
Victory gave Rapture
   – the best last half sandwich so perfect enough –
away,
goading,

> *"Say wheres across da track. Swear it.*
> *Tell what's 'round the corners."*

Eyes rhapsodized,
   beyond exhilaration,
   in unmitigated nirvana,
Someone devoured cinnamon and cotton candy corn flakes
   on rye.
Fresh, without rules, savory, magnificent;
   consuming it,
   guzzling,
   devouring it like soup;
...belching ecstatically before reimbursing devilishly,
   "Chickens."

> *"Chickens?"*

   "Chickens."

> *"Chicken-chickens?"*

   "Chick,
   chick,
   chick,
   chick,
   chick-ens, Baby."

> *"...Chickens.*
> *Umph.*
> *... Chickens."*

Trekking away, confusion
   – watching giants diminish;
   distance come near –
contemplated,

> *"One most original,*
> *tasteful, gratifying,*
> *... gratifying."*

Seasonably stronger, hereafter more focused,
   things familiar distorted.
   Strange turned customary.

Perhaps for reassurance, to the magic corn was recited
   "A - I - A - I - M."

Searching continued
   – alone, unstoppable –
rivaling Miss Ma'am's pursuance
   – consuming, maddening.
   "Ground for damnation,"
she grumbled so worried, laughing nervously.

> *"Things will be different now,"*
lectured reality.
> *"And never the same,"*
maturity affirmed.

> *"Responders? Where y'all at? 'Cross the*
> *track is where ... is ... 'round the corner?*
> *How ya get ratified? Who named the*
> *numbers? And seriously, who is you?"*

Unable to lie, one confessed,
> *"What a hard question.*
> *I'm thinking."*

* * *

6.
Rouge, Mascara and Dupery

On Happy Birthday, they
    – down the woodchip avenue,
    pass the molehill maze,
    near the magic corn –
discovered a loveliest being,

                                  singing with dancing
   cheerfully
               skipping with laughing
                           wildly,
        happily
                  swinging a suitcase,
   stuffed and floral.

   "I am Aman-da.
   Cute as a pan-da.
   Off to peep a gan-da
      at
   what's across the track."

Cloaking grotesque disfigurements and bazarre malformations,
    blush, desire and innocence painted her irresistible.
Coyness sensed a rival.

While others imagined cake,
mirth and laughter questioned her destination.
Track crossings loathe baggage, they'd heard.

She
    carefree, intriguing, in rat pee scented elbow gloves;
    switching, rolling, shaking her rump to
    plunkdi, plunkdi, hump bumpti, rhythms;
    strutting her – dipping her – throwing her stuff,
answered matter-of-factly, reading an emergency evacuation map.

    "This journey starts with a map and a note,
    with an ultimate goal in mind.
    Around the corner and over the track,
    a chest of wonders awaits my find."

                "Hey now!"

    "Filled with peace
    filled with love
    filled with happiness
    most desirably
        filled with success,
    this chest of wonders awaits me."

                "G'on, girl!"

    "Though this journey is long
    I have to stay strong
    to find what I long,
    around the corner,
        over the track."

Overshooting willpower,
    arousal turned smitten.
The others? Green.

Love, devoted and eternal
    – shedding folly and adolescence –
begged her company, boarding too, the magic corn.

Together, they soared
      behind the pompous,
    against the preposterous,
    atop the melodic,
    beneath the austere;
      beside the amazing,
    amidst the ecstatic,
    beyond the bodacious,
    to dreams far and near.

But,
    not around the corner;
certainly,
    not over the track.
No outhouses, no lasting peace, no comfort,
no chick, chick, chick-ens.
                "Nothing."

Alas, her compass
    – a crystal ball –
sucked.

Whereabouts uncertain, she devised,
    "I'll stand on your toes to see what's around the corner and over
    the track."

Everyone – entwined ill-timed – were sighted by
Her Forlornship, Miss. Erika the Elusive,
    forever memory-tending absent discernible spirit or soul,
    mothering six orphaned puppies,

a tarnished gold tooth peeping through self-talking lips.
Surely it was she, suspicion speculated –
   legend-billed half third cousin to
      a broken hearted friend of
      a down trodden comrade of
      a long forgotten acquaintance,
      draped – naps to bunions – in despair.

Probing politely over trollies passing loudly,
           "Where is 'round da corner?"
hoping she stomached strangers.

She heard nothing. Louder.
           "Where is 'round da corner?!"
And louder the rumble.

           "Where! Is! 'Round! Da! Corner!!"

She, demoralized by sudden screaming
   – in storied mushy hullabaloo –
answered reciting a bedpan cleaning guide:
   "The hours pass, the days pass, even months pass and
   I can't get you out of my head."
           "Us? Which one?"
   "You can never truly forget your first love,
   and even though I've found someone else,
   I will never forget you."
           "They say I look like my dad.
           Course, I never seen him? So..."
   "You were everything to me and I hurt you."
           "I think I'm like my uncles?"
   "Forgive me for all the pain I caused you."
           "Seem like they was so many?"
   "I will hold a space for you in my heart."
           "One aun'ie, she told one, she say,
           she'll whack his arm off
           if she catch us in bed again."
   "I feel disappointed in love, and all I do to smile..."

"She say flattery get ya nowhere."

"and all I do to smile..."

"And stop all the time seeing red?"

"and all I do..."

*"Had gold teefs, sho' did. Burns
everywhere. Gimps and stuff."*

"is think back at when I held you in my arms,"

"Like...um..."

"loving each other."

"...you?"

Their cherished companion,
    love of their lives,
their sugar-lips,
    doll-face,
    cutie patootie,
    tootsie-wootsy...
    "Your doodle-bug?"

"My rumpy-diddle."
"My honeytoast."
"My sweetie lamb."

Their rib,
Their flame,
Their shmoopsie-poo scrutinized them,
    cheeks – scorching firebrick – steamed streaming tears.
Vexation's face
    – knowing firebricks' burn –
matched her disillusion.

    "You said I was first,"
she cried.

"And you were,"
desperation replied.

Snippily, flippantly, arrogance sighed,
    "I was talking to her."

          * * *

7.
Fugue with Roaches in AB Negative

Solitude
    – not knowing why –
noticed molehills multiply randomly,
nameless,
    except the newest,
covering old bones,
    hadn't played Itsy Bitsy Spider in years.

Seclusion,
    packing them excessively,
    smoothing them,
    sweeping them perfect with a strip quilt broom
    – not gloomy, just
        ... distant
        ... detached
        ... mismatched –
spotted abnormal tints nearby with no one to know their value.

Loneliness
    – exhibiting the finest home training –
graciously ignored them,
then
    – whole gang of adjuncts gallivanting elsewhere –
tailed a trail of pale unruly hares
             "*Rabbits*"
or rabbits to an iridescent door once rejected –– open.

Stealing in,
life ambushed his void.
    Excitement appeared
        – scattin' rifts over nitrate bases.
    Opportunity surfaced
        – sporting vibrant enticements,
        pulsing,
        throbbing;
    Freedom emerged
        – struttin' 'n strollin' to slow flowing beats;
all lit dimly by a wood veneer console,
    scratched,
    tobacco scarred,
    projecting ...
    "*Storms. Storms.*"
                "*Storms?*"

But,
chameleon temptations revealed themselves.
Unknown spaces debuted in bright brilliant tapestries.
Things never done, hoped or dreamed
    availed themselves.

Arose a soulful rhapsody – notions and ideas
    intense,
    symphonic,
    antiphonal,
    pulsing.

Commenced unmilled secrets,
     laughters,
delicious sounds,
beautiful smells,
wonderful tastes and visions.

Life overflowed with endless parties,
     pre-parties,
     after parties.

The world became the after party of all after parties
with blow pops for everyone dancing naked
without a care about rhythms.

"Miss. Ma'am say the one know 'bout
storms get 'cross da track."

Countless legs, sundry hands enveloped him.

"But oh, what a day so promising,"
surmising an evanescent rainbow's bounty.

"Is this 'round da corner!"

Through pungent haze,
     inharmoniously,
manlike reflections – a trio – crooned,
     "No, my friend. There, the grass is stronger."

Disappointment overamplified birthed exasperation.
"Well, how ya' get there?"

Sneering anxious tenor soloed,
     "Fool, yo' punk ass ain't getting 'round no damn corner
     'til you slip cross the damn track."

Exasperation overboiling forged a fugue.

(Grandioso)   *"Again the damn track?*
                               What damn track!
                               I ain't seen na'on damn track.
                               Where the hell be a track? Show me."

Suave,
confident,
honeytoned
    "Come here, my brother,"
another
    – a baritone –
appealed in a lower key.
    "Discover, determine, live.
    Poverty born, raised by neglect,
    life, I spied around the corner.
    There still, it awaits you."
                               "But damn where?"

Chuckling garnished with staccato grace notes sang,
    "Where? Hear that? He say where. Look'a here..."
    "Wait a minute. Close your eyes; open your mind.
    Between worse and better, then and now;
    without past nor present it lies, here and there."

                               "But, do I get there, how?"

    "Get where, Fool? Damn."
Searching pockets of poker chips clicking like castanets,
    "if ya' can't see it, try this."

(Forte a animato)   *"Wow! Yeah! Cool! Righteous!*
                               Loud! Live! Rolling! Where da track?"

Dissonant responders droned off beat,
        "Caution – peril – caution – peril –"

In empty spaces whimpers sprouted –– sopranos and altos
somewhere anonymous.

Terse foot-tapping bass
crunched dead roaches,

> *"Patience. Sniff the track. Relax. Smoke it."*
> > *"Mmm. Bitter sweet like recent*
> > *separation. More please?"*
>
> *"Yes, my friend.*
> *Your father gives the world to you.*
> *Ours makes us cope and make do.*
> > *So,*
> *taste the corner for only one shoe.*
> *To smell it? Inhale it? That cost two."*
> > *"Both shoes? ... Okay."*

(Crescendo poco a poco)
> > *"My cousin Yolanda skipped over the*
> > *track ... so we can be free?"*
>
> *"Over the track is love, peace and unity."*
> *"Yeah. G'on join her. Swallow somma this. Shirt please."*
> > *"Sent back a letter say, 'round the*
> > *corner, over the track lies uncertainty*
> > *waiting to be savored in the dusk.'*
> > *What that mean?"*
>
> *"The track travels the world, My Brother. Surrender that belt and*
> *every corner becomes adventure."*
> > *"I like adventure, but trains coming.*
> > *The rumble. The bells. Hear 'em?"*
>
> *"Pass 'em, Man. Use this. Hurry."*

Slipped hand shaving rocks severed an ear.

> *"Sorry."*
> > *"More. Please."*
>
> *"Look at him. More?"*
delighted the tenor.
> *"Double dare ya to try somma this."*

Ruptured lighter torched fingers, legs, torso.

"Uo-oh."

"Got AB?"

Denied.

Begging, beseeching, prayerful petitioning
    -- altos, sopranos
... sopranos and altos.

Desperate for more,
he
   – despite the return of awaited seabirds –
cooked rapidly sandwiches succulent,
   nourishing,
   exquisite,
   unsigned
  – one, three, tens, many –
each a masterpiece consumed ferociously.

   "Damn! This ho' the sandwich man."
   "My brother. Oh, my brother."
   "Brutal. Scandalous."

Gladness tried, but needle prick pained, he cringed.

"They say over the track be a new life,
triumph for the family –"

"Yes, run. A new experience; new decision to make;
a new story to be lived. Run!"

Pleading echoed,
   hollers bellowed,
screams swelled from anonymous places
-- sopranos and altos.
   Sopranos only.
   ... One soprano
   ... None.

The Sandwich Man

(Furioso)   *"They say life and opportunity be*
                             'round the track / over the corner?"

        "Faster. G'on. You almost there."
                             "Trying ... I'm trying."
tripping,
toppling a lavender recliner.

        "Harder! Try! More?"
                             "See it; can't reach it? Help please."
begging,
trembling.
        "To buy what you need, say what you see."
                             "Buildings in bright reds and blues?
                             Tire shops, repair shops flashing reds
                             and blues. But the big corn's coming
                             and trains. I hear 'em."
heaving ash gray snot ...
                             "Please...More..."
hurling crimson vomit.

        "Attention traveler: Your journey is over. Get out."
                             "Wait!"
        "Gotta make a block. Bye! Hey! Tell ya poppa
        – our poppa, uncle, whatever we calling him –
        payback is a bitch."
                             "Please!!!..."

Well now,
through tear-stained windows
sunshine watching the whole thing
        couldn't wait to tell the moon, and...

...And sadness,
sang the responders' heart...and...

and...

and suddenly ...

...and sated,

...and silence.

* * *

8.
Plaid Poltergeists

Twitch.
Heartbeat.

Inhale. Exhale.

Overhung.
Overslept.
Overpassed.

Maybe morning came,
    deep sky blue slow dancing with rhythmic clouds.

Inhale. Exhale.

...rumble...fading...

Inhale.
Yarn.

Older eyes opened. Darkness gone.
Two darned rabbits or hares sniffed his face.
    "U" | *"the fool"* | *"looking"* | *"for the corner?"*
they inquired brazenly.
    "You trying" | *"to cross"* | *"them tracks?"*

    "You!"

Seeing no one,
    "You know U" | *"don't ya?*
he wondered who's asking.
    "What?" | *"You can't see?"*

In disbelief, he stared. Inhale.

    "Hey, we ain't the one" | *"on the ground"* | *"butt naked."*
    "Is you" | *"the one broke"* | *"into the"* | *"bone closet?"* | *"Or
out?"*

On cue, dead people in raincoats appeared,
above him – respected men;
about him – successful men;
aside him – ghosts of men once hoped to be;
    looking away after petting the rabbits
    ...or hares.

Rummaging for galoshes, clean underwear
    – bag empty, they too, gone –
he scrambled into cronyism's karma.
Someone mighty with a new friend approached.

Rabbits laugh clairvoyantly.
    Breathe. Cough.
These did.

    "Better get 'round that corner" | *"soon as you can,"*
goaded calmly, ingesting the absolutely singular last half sandwich.
    "Stunning." | *"Scrumptious."* | *"Most lovely."*

He solicited,
    "Dan?! How's it going guy,"
ignoring all critics
    – crooks, allies, the fluffy, enormous –
maneuvers years ago attempted.

They warned,
    "Okay," | *"rejection corrodes."* | *"Yeah."* | *"And corrosion skins"*
    | *"bakes"* | *"stews"* | *"feels terrible."* | *"Ouch!"* | *"Unlearned
    lessons"* | *"kill."*

                        *"We - I - know U. Wouldn't be headed
                        'round the corner, would ya'?"*

Danny shooed him.

                        *"We're - I'm heading that way. Can I
                        tag?"*

Waving him off,
mischief reading an inverted cookbook,
muffled with baritoned breath,

    *"Saggy, like a desiccated leaf,
        she hangs on my shoulder,
        drunken until drowsiness,
        slurred speech and slurred steps
        scratching and sniffing the concrete."*

                        *"Miss. Ma'am say the one know 'bout
                        the storm get 'cross the track."*

    *"Laughter,
        in the most slovenly manner possible,
        uncoordinated and feral,
        inspiring the monster within,
        deep and ragged, I laugh too.*

                        *"Miss. Ma'am, she told my cousin
                        Yolanda 'nem the one know 'bout the*

storm, they can ... they gon get 'cross the
track."

There's no fear of the deepest dark unknown,
      flippantly blown away,
      song and cheer lighten the path,
      the midnight moon clears,
      and the stars shine bright."

                    "Miss. Ma'am, uhm,
                    she say - uh..."

"Taking a swish of bootleg coconut juice,
      she grins at me,
      its lust, and its torturous,
      but swiftly so, I whisk her away.

Scandalous."

                    "We know A and I and U and M, and
                    Miss. Ma'am, say...uhm...Hey! Miss.
                    Ma'am, she ..."

Around the curious,
      under the prudent,
            into the crowd,
                  Gone.

                    "...The future,"
hummed quietly to the magic corn,
                    "somewhat unclear –
                    Wonder whatever I'm gonna find..."
      "Jealous?"
the darned inquired,
licking barbecue sauce from crooked hand stitches.

Angrily, he scorned,
                    "Y'all been 'round the corner?!

Y'all know what's over the track?!"
"Yeah." | "Of course" | "Got sweethearts there," | "big purple
cows," | "poor folks," | "Black folks," | "green and silver folks," |
"the unknown," | "the 'hood," | "the yard," | "downtown," | "the
east part of town," | "and west," | "hope," | "success" | "and a
big messy change," | "U" | "but good."

Skeptical,
reluctant, he...
   paused.
He...
   thought.

He retaliated,

            "Man, please.
            I been lied to, too many times?
            Cows ain't purple, them's bulls."

"Don't call us man, man." | "We're bunnies." | "Uh-huh" |
"Lovable loafers." | "Better tell him." | "Purple is" | "what we
want it" | "to be." | "Who didn't tell him?" | "They told him." |
"Did they?"

Sigh.

Slipping away, collecting dust, canvassing reality with canvas ears,
   "And mom and pops," | "life," | "road kill," | "the crib," |
   "uncertainty," | "the me I'd like to be," | "southside," | "Mom
   and Pops, ... did I say that already?" | "Think you said that
   already." | "Did I?" | "Maybe".

* * *

9.
Fresh Air

Over time, mammoth oceans,
    a.k.a. Lake Rudolph, a.k.a. a lily pond,
    hero to countless puddles,
perished restoring time-scarred images, resisting
    hostile hair – hideous wind driven tumbleweeds;
    belligerent beards – aggressive, scraggly, gray patched.
Every ghastly strand on ghostlike heads
    – each pitying identical others;
    each mirroring a mind overburdened –
taunted unlimited barbers,
    promise-filled barbers,
    hungry barbers,
    barbers pursuing fame. But,
previous defeats overruled hopes of splendor-reaped fortunes.

They heard,
    "Arrive styling"
morph to
    "style upon arrival"
morph to
    "consider grooming if ya' get there."
Replying to all,
                "Why bother?"

Even food
   – rarely plentiful lures irresistible –
everyone repelled,
    ever a troupe united, tenacious,
    their bond insolvable,
    a wall impenetrable
    – until –
come an iceberg day polluted with frost
one, surrendering, endured everyman's predestined pilgrimage.
   His Mecca: The Liberty Hair Emporium.

In that hallowed temple where proud men go,
    over buzzing clippers hustling,
    around shaving cream's reek,
masculinity's typical theme and variations
already present, queued, heavily coated in eminence,
    sermonized,
    editorialized,
    criticized,
    aggrandized
every nothing
   – under, between, behind –
anywhere pettiness hides;
    prompting, prodding,
    poking the lone defector.

Studying Liberty's ceiling, he blurted,
       "Fresh air. More fresh air."

A startled jheri curl slung relaxer on a conk,
almost started a brawl – but it's cool – no scrapping at the Liberty.

A one-armed barber – old, uneasy – opened windows.

Shivering in linen and thinly clad,
the turncoat waiting placidly,
    dodged inquisitions of immodest men endlessly testing all
    mankind's pecking order.

      The Sandwich Man

Women desperate to be so meddlesome, dream.
Rocking, trembling, staring at Liberty's floor,
> *"Boysenberry. Boysenberry.*
> *More fresh air."*

Dreadlocks nudged a 'frohawk.

A one-arm barber, obese, started fans.

Overzealous youngsters yearning experience needled,
> *"How much you tipped 'round the corner, Pops? Still try'na find*
> *them tracks?"*
> *"Find 'em? Damn. Hear a bell, feel a rumble, get out the way*
> *'cause there they is."*

Veterans laughing, *"More fresh air?"* stirred the next contest.
> *"Look at him. See? Look at him."*
> *"I heard his old man invented the corner*
> *– all the tipping he done*
> *– burying all them not-borns."*
> *"What? Abortions?"*
> *"Man, please. Weren't nobody wearing coats back then."*
> *"I heard he made 'em drink turpentine and put leeches up they*
> *jelly."*
> *"That's crazy."*
> *"Maybe that's why he's crazy."*
> *"Maybe."*

He blinked, studying weed on black velvet embellishing the place.

Another barber said,
> *"Next."*

Bleached high top requested a fade.

> *"They say his ol' man swanked him too."*
> *"D-a-a-a-m-n."*
> *"Slipped 'round the corner 'fo they caught him. Probably*
> *somewhere living large."*
> *"Yeah? Well, I ain't gon lie..."*

One arm barber, paused to listen.

> *"if I knew his ass, I'll soak every dime he got, then bust him first*
> *time he can't deliver."*
> *"I heard he done every crime been wrote, then made up some."*
> *"How he end up here?"*
> *"Camouflage, masquerade."*
> *"Jazz man talking 'bout making it big. Stole Pop's money, went*
> *'round the corner, ain't been seen again."*
> *"Pops had money?"*
> *"Eh... Any of that true? That's why you try'na find them tracks?"*

Deploying silence
   – a weapon potent but unstable –
he divulged nothing, hoping
> *"indignance is indigo, like ..."*

hollering,
> *"Bulls! Bulls! Bulls! Bulls!"*

Barber's only hand gently, but grating, settled him.

Bunch'a twists checked the set-up in case things change – have to
slice somebody.

> *"Y'all joking, but they say the track refers to time, as in a bit of*
> *waiting time."*
> *"More like wasting time."*
> *"I think it's what happened a while ago."*
> *"No, that's wrong. It's a new journey that will soon begin."*
> *"Always talking out the back of y'all's head. What you got, Prof?"*
> *"The corner speaks of time. The track is a place."*
> *"Scandalous. Scandalous."*
> *"I think the track is a goal – a destination."*
> *"Yes, My Brother, a dream divided by social status, monetary*
> *value, racial profile."*
> *"No it ain't. The track is like the future, the past, most*
> *importantly, the present."*
> *"So, what is is what's to come? That's what ya saying?"*
> *"I think a successful launching waits around the corner."*
> *"Yeah, let you tell it."*

"He saying it's a simile."
"Man, get out'ta here. Semi my butt."
"Why you ain't talking, Pops? You mad?"
"They dream smashing. Look at him. Look at him."
"When you turn the corner don't forget us. Okay?"
"Man stop," Someone laughed, *"this fool ain't never getting*
    'round no corner."
"Don't believe 'em Pops. All you need is a pipe and a suit. Can't
    get there 'less you look right."

He blinked.

"Next!"
Bunch'a cucabugs requested waves on the top with curvy cornrows
    on both sides wrapping 'round to a shag in the back.
Two beards and a goatee laughed.

"Maybe it's a semi-metaphor of community divisions
    representing the death of you and me."
"Yes, my brother! A metaphor based on streets, town dwellings;
    meaning life and opportunity."
"The track or corner?"
"One say track; one say corner. What you say, Pops?"

Toilet paper unwrapping his neck, he
    – grateful but unable to pay –
hastily, defiantly
threw a sandwich with grape and jazzberry jam...
                    "So perfect enough?"
against the barber's wall, proclaiming triumphantly,
                    "Liberty!"

Vividness restored where fresh air faded;
    proud, gloating, feeling squared,
into a day still polluted, he scooted,
covered in fresh air.

                    * * *

10.
Who and Whosoever

Gathered high atop a molehill,
 a congress of distinguished oddballs
 watched darkness' stellar cast milk their curtain call.
Each night they muse
 bemuse
 amuse spectators
 shining – flickering – unrehearsed.
They come, go,
 come, go
 – a mesmerizing company so perfect enough –
hypnotic,
captivating,
inspiring,
silent
 – the stars, too –
except
 somewhere reclusive,
 somewhat restless,
rehashing repeatedly, remarkably off-key,

"A new life, new time, a new laugh..."
squalled.

Vexed, Meister Moodiness groaned.
Beatings stopped when music died, and he
    – mortician to old trombones –
lacked love for nostalgia.
Echoing distant thunder,
he
      caustic, comfortably wry,
                  "Responders! Neighbors! Friends!"
      pessimistic, dry,
rumbled,
                "Where'd y'all find that song?"

For a mob of moldy responders,
    mildewed neighbors,
    musty friends
    – each attentive but not the singer –
only Captain Reticence draped in manatee feathers, replied.

Faithful to none,
    Doubt Man,
resident artisan of spit flavored mud pies
    – despising riddles –
quibbled acrimoniously,
               "If not you, then who?"
suspecting King Schizod,
    ever picking licorice lice from someone's hair.

Over and over, a surrogate / telepath / ventriloquist,
    – querying soundlessly if this coming day so wondrous
    holds a ticket home –
hopeful, distant, A Capella, continued:
    "A new life, new time, a new laugh, new cry;
    New life, new time, a new laugh, a new cry;
    New life, a new ..."
                "time, laughing –– yeah, yeah, got it."

"Mm-hmm, maybe."

The Composure twins
    – Serenity and Docility –
felt the temperature drop.

Yielding, yet jaded, Uncle Cynicism rummaging clues where
Cousin Rage couldn't reach
    – under daffodil beds,
    behind dandelion doors,
    along orphaned trails,
    between friendly oaks, merciful willows –
summonsed wrathfully,
                "Is we close?"
discounting a rising dew point.

Fog's creep began.
        "Maybe."
             "Maybe?"
murmured gruffly.

             "Maybe. Umph. Maybe."
    remembering,
for things unknown, harsh hands tortured Miss. Ma'am.
For skills not owned, callous hands singed and scorched him;
then too, hearing,
    "maybe."

Everyone's list of culprits differed but all suspected Someone.

Persuaded loyal comrades concealed reconnaissance,
prey stalked prey-stalking prey,
    causing deepening mist, discoloring their day; remembering,
for who he couldn't be corrupt hands defiled him,
blaming him for status not achieved.

             "Say,"
trap baiting,

"how would you know?"

Clarity's fog
    – strangely blinding –
freed the unforeseen.
Demanding respect,
    one responder ever unheeded
unleashed wisdom's might.
        "Around the corner, over the track,
        stronger-willed it waited."
            "...It?"
        "Viciously consuming another, I feared he thought it
        was me."
            "...He?"
        "Fast as I could, I ran.
        They chased me,
        caught me,
        crushed me."
            "They? Why? What? Who?"
        "Death...and life. Bliss and misery."
            "And you?"

Candidly,
       "You."

Panicked, Prince Aspiration,
known for courage and valor
    – out from adventure,
    far from sensibility –
rushed terrified,
    frenzied,
    anywhere,
    everywhere;
scuttling everyone
aimlessly without destiny,
    troubled, unfocused, tormented, furiously,
    round and round, round, round,
    scooting – scooting – scooting – exhausting
at the Fabulous Wine Emporium,

refuge of everyone's sweet Aunt LaShiya,
    indigent but everyone's treasure;
    pipe smoking,
    one dress having,
    grateful lauder of a piggy pink chair;
    guardian of a childless manger;
    frail, failing,
        despite-it-all God praiser,
    foot patting, handwaving,
        body-rocking head swayer.
Some recalled when
    "...she knew laborers fresh off the ferries before they caught the
    trolleys had the most money."
           "Yeah. Every Monday, Tuesday, Thursday, Friday."
    "Always talking 'bout leaving soon's she find her cross."
Rebuked, deprived
    – still nourishing dreams of others;
    intrinsic dreams previously her own.
Wretchedly delusional
    – happy and mad;
sometimes dreaming of having enough;
    ever fashioning a masterpiece day for going home.

To this mindless wretch
    – former shame-bringer to good men's names –
breathlessly Contentment pleaded,
                    "Been meaning to stop by, but ...
                    been so busy, I...
                    know I ain't been around, but...
                    time kept getting away, I...
                    don't wanna impose, but...
                    kin'a in a rush, so....
                    can you tell me what's 'round the
                    corner?"

Convinced they never met,
            "Liar!"
King Outrage snitched.

Aunt Shya, ancient, deranged,
    born blind, bashed deaf,
sensing a presence
    – mysterial, magnetic –
bowed to fantasies silvery, savage, grey ... like ...
    "stormcloud."
Sure as he knew A-I-A-I-U-M
    she knew stormcloud.

Treading gingerly,
quoting memorized coupons and flyers,
    "I
    just
    wanna talk to him ...and...
    see 'bout his family, ...and...
    let him know I care 'cause that's..."
examining cautiously,
    "That's just who I am.
    And tell him ...
    don't waste no time with a careless girl.
    And tell him never let nobody boss his world."

Leering onlookers queried insipidly,
            "Can dry riverbeds smell water?
            Do leafless trees break wind?"

In a wasted cradle,
    wrinkled hands trembling near plaid rabbits;
    fingers gnarled, fragile,
    rummaging shreds of tiger's eye
inspected blueberry diapers with peach rhinos and sea green sheep,
    hand-sewn crookedly,
tattered,
still folded,
still dry.

Never quick witted, Lil' Innocence stared loudly,
            "Ya think stars know they neighbors?"

and louder,

> *"In what tongue do mockingbirds think?"*

Her abandoned mind rabidly dusting thought caverns;
 – memory crypts allusive to others;
 as loneliness screamed quietly,
 Who's there? Any news? –
while audibly she rambled,

> *"I wanna always remind him of his worth,*
> *and make sho' he know he can always strive forth.*
> *I'ma try to kiss his lil' cheek and make him smile*
> *and make him love staying with me awhile.*
> *But right now they just babies and can't understand.*
> *But long as they my nephews*
> *I'll always encourage 'em under any circumstance."*

Black widow spider wondering where to bite her
paraded over shoeless feet.

> *"Nephews? How many?"*

Blunted sword trailed eight tiny legs
around blisters and sores, once to the white meat.

> *"Why do wrong be friendly"*

he wondered

> *"and right so shy?*
> *How come seeds know what to be?"*

Spider halting,
 challenged the sword near varicose veins
 pulsing irregular ancestral rhythms,
 syncopated beats like jazz.
 He hated jazz.
 Harsh hands made raucous passionate jazz,
 but beatings stopped when the music stopped,
> *"Killing it! Killing it!"*
revelers once shouted.

Swatting the monster,
   stabbing it,
   killing it,
he had no love for nostalgia.

Her foot, too, deeply gored,
agony, angst and reminiscence screamed,
snatched the squared sword and...,
   "Hallelujah!"
                    "What's ya favorite word?
                    Who named the numbers?"

Whisperer to time and salamanders,
she
   – joyful,
   knowing,
   laughing,
   toothless –
victoriously declared,
   "Whosoever! Whosoever! A new life."
                    "A new time."
   "A new laugh."
                    "A new cry."
He with one ear and her none heard all responders perish.

But, oh wondrous day so twisted.

Under ma'velous skies arrived a smile new to angst-filled lips.
Sightless eyes locked on him.
Rocking stopped.
Foot patting stopped.
        "Impediments and unused weights,"
came to mind, dragging
        "days not hollow, where did you go?"

Her long awaited suitor welcoming:
   "Step on in this chariot – Darling – neon with wings,
   smartly groomed and all fixed-up for changing things.

The foolish get marv'lous;
the mauv'lous, golden.
Got seats for whosoever, come paupers, come kings."

Draping her with a strip quilt cloak,
Humanity Man
   – kissing hope-giving eyes goodbye –
whispered silently,
   "A perfect enough day for going home?"

Ethos translated:
         "Maybe around the corner,
         away from the situation eagles cry.
         Perhaps dreaming of success, happiness, love, blue
         birds fly. Sometimes, getting closer to something
         over the tracks – or someone – caution ponders why."

Boggled, Meister Moodiness studied,
               "The responders live?"
   "We live. Yes. We live."

* * *

11.
To the Zoo

When the magic corn ate everyone;
    the poet,
    the slut,
    somebody, everybody;
when every seat filled -
    a dancer,
    the drunk,
    sitting next to someone;
when children were quiet,
    rabbits quieter,
    puppies left alone;
a pastor, the gambler,
    a barber, everyone
saw an eggshelled pilot in eggplant garb step aboard smiling.
Someone whispered,
    "danger"

                             "danger"
         "Stranger"
      "Danger!"   *"Stranger"*
"Danger!   *"Danger*   *"Danger"*
  "Danger" *"Stranger!"* *"Stranger"* **"Danger!"**   *"Danger"*
"Stranger"   *"Danger"*   *"Danger"*   *"Stranger!"*
    "Danger!!" *"Stranger"* *"Danger"*   *"Danger! Stranger"*
Stranger Danger   *Danger* *Stranger*   *Danger!*

"Danger"   "Danger"   "Danger"   "Stranger"

                            * * *

12.
The Faithful

First,
    gracefully,
    lightly,
        whiff.

Way down by the creek a light cut on;
    caught Deacon Daniel – lost a shoe climbing out a window.

Wisp,
trippingly...
           (Sniff)
                        "Banana nut toast?"
          "Yeah."

Someone unlatching church doors,
    left hooked a torn screen,
        for the time being.

The Sandwich Man

Tenderly, peacefully,
whiffs gently waft.

>>> *"Uhm. Garlic toast!"*
>>> *"Yeah! buttered."*

...flurries...

>>> *"And juice? Orange?"*

...flurries, willowy...

>>> *"Fresh squeezed ... and coffee"*

...flurries waving...

>>> *"...medium roast."*
>>> *"Mm-hmm."*

Warm wisps woo-f-f-f'd.

Window fan across the street came on;
    and one next door.
Yesterday's wash still sagging three weary lines
    swayed...
Whoosh.
    ...and swung
on ceaseless puffs.

>>> *"Fresh cinnamon rolls, Baby.*
>>> *"Man!"*

Someone set out offering plates,
    a kitchen chair at the piano;
        draped sofas with table cloths;

Woof-f-f, boldly.
Whoosh.

>>> Replaced felt weed with The Last Supper;
>>> hid dead lamps where bones once lived.

Zephyrs.

"Grits?"

"Cream of Wheat."

"No. Grits."

"Cream of Wheat."

"Them is grits!"

"Cream -- Of -- Wheat!!

Swirls

"Wait."

Gusts

"Oatmeal (sniff) with maple and brown sugar."

"...and butter?"

Gallant gusts, brash.

"Yes, on...um..."

Tiny dust devils rise and die.
Uncut grass and wildflowers dance.
Child somewhere didn't wanna get up
   – caught a whooping.

Strong gusts. Robust.

"Baked ham!"

"Whaaat? Nooo! Not, ham. Baked?"

Someone readied the kitchen for covered dishes;
   set out napkins,
   paper plates,
   paper cups and foil,
      lots of foil,
      gotta have foil.

"Peaches, pineapples, plumbs, prunes, pecans."

"Yummy!"

Come a squall billowy,
   blustery,
gloved hands changed a hat picked last night
   and purse,
   pumps,
   earbobs and rouge.

Tree limbs rustled,
    swished,
    whooshed.
Early feet hastened under old bird nests accustomed to whooshing.
Nests of younger mothers languished on the ground.

Woof-f-f
                "Hot biscuits with blackberry syrup."
                      "Hush!"
                "Warm apple turnovers."
                    "Yes, Lord!"

Someone set out the pastor's robe.
Gales, who-o-o-d, wo-o-o...
             "Eggs."
                    "Scrambled?"
             "Omelet."

Whole bag of peppermints filled an empty purse.
Ribbons replaced rubber bands on restyled pony tails.

Ish-h-h.
             "Links..."
                    "Come on, now"
Zish-h-h.
             "Bacon..."
                    "Preach!"

Tish-h-h.
             "Fried chicken.
             Fried pork chops.
             Fried lamb chops."
Ushers passed out fans and programs.

With least movement possible
   – keep from getting hot,
   no arm swinging,
   no fast going –

high heels carried a bible filled with blank notes, and
   baked beans in an empty pot.

Along came
   a bass player running late,
   had to fix strings broke last night at the juke house.

Along came
   a peach cobbler,
   chocolate cake,
   four new puppies.

Whaff.
Hoos-s-s.
Whaf-f-f.
               "Jambalaya..."
                        "Good goobedywop!"
               "Boudin, dirty rice, shrimp gumbo..."
                        "Help me somebody b'fo I do some'um!"

Collard greens whistling,
   green peas whipping,
   cornbread, yams
       rough riding rivers of wild vapory winds,
       burden bearers of Sunday's sounds:
   crackling candles,
   un-tuned piano.
Two sisters grabbed the same tambourine.
The choir rose in rose robes belting
   Come Thou Almighty King
as wind gusts swung the screen door loose
declaring the Kingdom, open.

Trolling their thistle stockade,
   observing the pious,
   admiring conviction,
   tacitly muttering
               "the faithful,"

malnourished heirs to a
    piggy pink chair,
    carrot stoop,
    empty closet for lifeless bones,
daily competed for waste
    – fresh or fermented –
typically,
losing to bums more virtuosic.

Sundays were different.
Matchless and plentiful is the garbage of saints,
    fashioning a quandary.

Skies darkened.
Drizzle washed the air.

The anguished ones
    – thirsting a sip of Ms. Ma'am's strength
    wondering could the faithful's goblet end a lifelong search –
demanded:
        "Follow 'em. Let's get in there. Join 'em."

The desperate ones
    – salivating leftovers,
    craving sacks of would've been trash –
having bared a fruitless week,
refused baring one day more.

        "They always bring out the leftovers,
        y'all. We staying put,"

balked Intrepidness.

        "And sometimes stuff for new
        sandwiches come?"

spoils worthy of combat.
    Lightening.
    Thunder.
    Deadlock.

Nosy, bigmouth, meddling canopy
    – always instigating;
    nurturing darkness –
flapped fiercely, inciting war.

But,
Miss. Ma'am's legacy prevailed.
Facing discord, often she blurted,
    "A lil' cream and chocolate make meat brown."
Everyone pretending to know what that meant,
    always compromised.

The hesitant ones
    – famished for hors d'oeuvres,
    knowing comrades craved soul food more –
remained, keeping watch.

The adventurous ones
    dapperly dressed in borrowed discards
hurried to feast with the faithful.
        "Who talk the right track more than the faithful?
        Who know corner turning more than them?"

Usher in elbow gloves welcomed them.

The faithful crammed
    on lumber sofas and a faded jade loveseat,
    praising in the key of see - aka "be sharp" -
rocked to soul bending rhythms,
    loud,
    pounding,
    bliss of the redeemed,
        swaying left
        swerving right
        shifting back
        swinging forth
    clapping, jumping, waving, stomping;
hats with feathers over fried hair,

blue hair, yellow, orange;
   clapping, jumping, waving, stomping;
sharkskin suits,
snakeskin belts,
alligator shoes,
brims creased and pinched;
   clapping, jumping, waving, stomping;
Guitar, drums and tambourines driving
   "a sho' nuff Holy Ghost party,"
                  "she would'da said,"
   clapping, jumping, waving, stomping,
      left
      and right
      and back
      and forth.

Praying glazed ceramic hands graced a makeshift alter
   – coffee table, strip-quilt covered.

The rostrum
   – a music stand –
   leaned.

Covered console
   – communion table –
   reeked of talcum powder.

A one arm pastor in dark purple cassock
   over plum clergy shirt,
   under violet robe,
   majestically adorned with silk orchid stole
reposed on velvet throne
   – recliner, secondhand, lavender.

Someone spinning in bewildering circles,
   – shouting expertly, free form, shrewdly –
guarded cash atop a warbly card table.

Lightening.
Thunder.
Hell raged as
    praising thunderously, hailing raged.

A wretched soul surrendered yelled,
                "What waits 'round the corner,
                Faithful?"

    "Salvation!"
The faithful cheered.
                "Who wants a bowl of eternal life?"

    "We!"
they begged together.
                "Hallelujah?"
he called.
    "Hallelujah!"
they answered.
                "Who wants to go now?"
Silence.

As buxom rain rode muscular winds,
in a tub they dunked him;
with warmed lard they doused him;
upon him they laid hands.

                "What's gonna be on the other side,
                Faithful?"
"The future church! Heaven! Hesperides! Jannah!
Moksha! ..."
Thunderbolts crackled.
            "Come again?"
"One day, we'll meet our savior: Brahma,
Chukwu, Confucius, Jesus..."
Twisters.
            "Unison and unity are just friends?"

Squeamishly, laggardly,
                "How do I get there?

Who name the numbers?"
wreckage, confusion, chaos, destruction.

"Chant."

"Confess"

"Meditate"

"Handle snakes"

"Tongue talk"

"Sing and dance"

"Kneel and pray"

"Shout"

"What if I simply believe?"

Discussion began.
Conflict ensued with arguments,
    insults,
    brawls,
    anarchy.
Loathing lightening and thunder unmuted,
back to a monsoon's safety they scooted,
    tacitly muttering,
                "The Faithful."

* * *

13.
Sandwiches, Y'all

Nature reduced them to singing:
> *"Sandwiches, y'all! Sandwiches for shoes!"*
> *"Tangerine with zucchini!"*
  to shotgun shells formerly unlivable,
  now vacant.

Neighbors and good times mostly gone,
  maybe around the corner, or
  over the track, maybe.

Bewildered,
  – their autumnal splendor a harvest nonexistent –
they huddled beneath a fearless bridge to futility
  – stalwart canopy reportedly cruel or worse.
They stared, hypnotized by A I U and M,
  damaged, still magical.

The Sandwich Man

Rising to power after daring's failed coup
Reluctance
    – disinclined sentinel of poverty's artistry –
obscurely watched comely-suited visionaries survey their
second-to-none collections:
    cardboard castle motifs;
    dumped necessities bending spaces;
    drifts of discarded fixer-uppers awaiting reclaim;
paucity's decor;
wealth of the abhorred.

Others sang relentlessly,
> *"Mustard and pear on pumpkin bread – Pumpkin*
> *bread! Bittersweet nutriments! Get some, gimmi*
> *some! Sandwiches y'all! Got sandwiches?"*

Resignation
    – never a participant –
> *"Don't pay me no mind, just looking,"*
noted bulldozers raze scarcity's renderings;
    ousted by
designers,
architects,
builders of nostalgia replace authentic ethos;
    ousted by
altruistic women, restless children boasting fashionable buckets
    planting witch hazels,
    turtleheads,
    red spider lilies;
yielding
    terra cotta art galleries garnished with
    silver chalice,
    French wine,
    cosmic latte.
But no sandwiches
    – no food or drink allowed.

"So wonderful, so necessary,"
groaned Submission, watching others' annihilation.

Their own riddance spared,
a gullible quest for 'round the corner rejoiced,
trumpeting,
    "Welcome, welcome, the gentry!..."
Ms. Ma'am's memory added,
 "...-fyers."

Elsewhere,
pomp and merriment welcomed a sparkling causeway,
where ferry horns, gulls, trolley rumbles kissed
  and were no more.

Ignoring that,
  expecting collaboration
they observed scholars arrive, philosophers come,
and lovers and painters with coffees and teas
  hearing rhapsodists make public their souls.

Over thistle wattle never passed,
one,
    "Ya think maybe I could just be back here?"
eavesdropped a mope-clad bard
 – Lady Anastacia –
croon others with her worry.

From a help wanted flyer she read,
 "Without him waking me up,
 is like waking up deceased, broken down."
      "Louder!"
 "Without him saying good night
 is like God himself, taking me,
 not waking me from slumber
 so that I may not see his loving face,
  or worse,
 hear his soft but manly voice,

to find encouragement or guidance
for my lonesome heart."
                    "What she say?"
"He is here in my heart
but we may not speak,
someone has taken him, my life.
My heart, now feeling as if my soul whisked away.
The one that makes me feel sentimental,
holding me in life's rough moments,
always there – a spirited loving man."
                    "It's upside down. Turn it over!"
"One day, I'll find you.
Until then, think of me, your love,
Forever."
Others marveling,
    enraptured by maxims,
    meters,
    meanings
swooned.

Chatting much too loud as usual,
rumor and opinion hypothesized,
                    "Didn't you use to go by Erika?"

Applauding such candor and repartee
    – so rich,
    so colorful –
impressionable crowds deified them and served them T.

Thereafter,
    – tolerated among loftyism's realm –
persistence proudly troweling everyone down new paths to failure.
    calamity whaling,
    blues picking,
    sandwich-making 'til fingers wept,
    unable to drop a half dollop more;
all gifted to unfruitfulness.

On dime here; nickel there.
    endurance prevailed.

Special order for
    "a little dollar bill"
                "One? Two? How much?"
produced regard for gold,
    independence,
    optimism.

Vintage doubt, reserved for special occasions argued,
              "Sandwiches. Just sandwiches, y'all.
              Tomato and salmon with arsenic."

* * *

14.
Wealth

All rare fortnights when cupboards filled,
Ms. Ma'am,
    – deposing empty wine jars,
    begging forgiveness –
would sigh so loudly enough in self defense,
    "Panties dropped like dollar bills rent cooperation."

Such laments overheard, the industrious one,
    pantyless,
dropped a little dollar bill
    on everything, everywhere,
discovering
    increased wealth increased friends.
Seasons overwrought with non-met necessities
    camouflaged greed and perfected imperfections.

Toxic thigh predators stalked,
one tapping his shoulder,
    "one, please."

Lust
    – cynical, reliving younger days –
bartered,
                    "And I'ma get what?"

She paused,
    "I know everything."
                "Everything?"
    "I can read,"
she whispered.

He gasped, pointing to the Magic corn,
                "What's that one, this and that?"
    "R - S - N"

Never knowing a real reader,
Condescension concealed his awe.
               "That's all ya got?"

Naiveté overwhelmed reason,
    "They're coming."
              "Who?"
    "I offer truth. They're coming."

He
– thinking her mad –
    "...They!"
she insisted,
unriddling his quandary.
    "Them,"
resolute,
enticing,
playful.

He
   – impressed by simplicity –
tickled her nose with a little dollar bill,
offering to place more elsewhere.
   Kickerless.
   Catchless.

She giggled perfectly.
Ms. Ma'am would have colored her smoke.

Others prone to larceny assembled, pining opportunity.

She
   – impressed by simplicity –
stayed for conversation,
   laughs,
   lunch.
Ms. Ma'am would have stuffed her nose with flattery, embroidered.

He
   – over dried neck bones, lavish spoils –
admitted pilfering dead squirrels' pecans, acorns.

She
   – wearing bubble gum jewelry,
   sipping vintage pot liqueur –
berated phony magnates, dream brokers.

He
offered them gold, silver.

Hunting exotic rabbits he confessed to theft:
   bras, dresses from sagging clotheslines worn to unsuspecting
   places infested with compliments and complements.

Louder she laughed.
Loudly he laughed,
   obsession dying his hair razzmatazz and folly.

His most treasured possession shared
    – a secret lullaby –
entranced her.

He
    – dancing, carousing in younger man's deportment –
exaggerated prowess,
inflated potential,
lied of achievements,
warmly greeting all plutocrats evading her shield;
    each receiving a little dollar bill and promises of full coverage.

    "Listen,"
she paused.
    "One gull, lost. They followed ferries to the trolley. Remember?"
        "Maybe."

To her,
sincerity whimpered,
            "What's your name?"
    "What would you like?"
            "...Sharmaine."
    "That's it!"
she laughed,
    discovering a stash of flawless sandwiches.

He laughed.
Friends laughed.
Masses laughed.
Hunger starved.

Hoping to patronize pay toilets,
    but neither having dime or penny,
gasping crowds dissolved.

She chuckled,
    "Where did it go?"

                                                   The Sandwich Man

"Over champagne and popstar
trimmings.   Someone wasted the rest."

"Told ya,"
she giggled.
"They came."
He
   – stowed behind bushes relieving himself,
   reciting gifts from her,
                "R-S-N-S-R-S-N..."
   already knowing the rest –
heard giggling change to song,
   his blessing,
   a lullaby,
strong but fading.

   "I look left.
   I turn right.
   Everything's new.
   Everything's bright.
   A future ahead
   that's somewhat unclear;
   I wonder what
   I will find here.
   A new life,
   a new time,
   a new laugh,
   a new cry;
   whatever it is
   bring it on.
   I love change
   and I love this song!"

Hearing only the crackle of leaves cleansing himself,
                "...Sharmaine?..."
he called.
Unexpected rain answered.
                "Responders?...

scalding him;

     ...Hey! Re!...

scolding him.

     ...They?!..."

       * * *

15.
Them

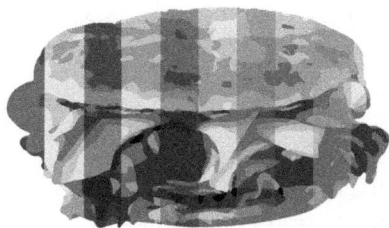

Near the winter of their winter
three
        – only three –
remained.

Wondering,
weltering,
withstanding,
withering,
        one wheedled,
        and wangled
        and waited.
The blameless and bifocaled went about their business.
The well begotten went about their business.

Watching waves of tinsel shoppers
    – tidings and cheer ignored;
    raspberry pipe wedged between wry lips –
another
    – unworried –
rested.
The beautiful, the bountiful went about their business.
Bisexual bowlegs went about their business.

Unwavering strip quilt warming their huddle,
    both squalid,
    oblivious,
    idle;
one joked of being so well-endured
    – slyly wooing the other.
Brawny women went about their business.
Bigoted men went about their business.

The other spurned such wicked advances
preferring to weep their unsalable wares
    – wrong turns,
    worthless dreams –
regaling the wraith of joy
    as
the big hearted,
big mouthed and
big headed bluntly
went blindly about their business.

                    "Always wasting my time."
was whined.
            "Well walk, why don't cha?"
warmongered.

The bashful
                "You worm."
Baronial
          "You wart."

bloodshot
>   *"... wino."*

bilingual
>   *"Chicken."*
>   *"What you say?"*
>   *"Chick,*
>   *chick,*
>   *chick,*
>   *"...Chick-en ... hmm."*

callously went about their business.

Yesterdays abundant,
tomorrows meager;
    uncertainties plentiful,
    achievements few;
carelessly weathered by a comfortless over caste,
    they,
waited so weighted of waste,
and ...
    just waited.

Bottomless bureaucrats went about their business,
Bipartisan bungaloids went about their business
while each
wallowing in lunacy's wilderness,
    slanderously walloped the other:

>   *"Weasel, you the one whinny and*
>   *weak."*
>   *"You would be what had you found the corner?"*
>   *"Why ya weather map always wrong?"*
>   *"And crossing them tracks would get you where?"*

As bakers and brick layers went about their business
and bootlegging bartenders went about their business.
wrangling of worldly wonders missed
    for not being wiser or better wardrobed,

they watched reality waltz by awash in waylays,
    white and wee.

Bank bosses,
broom handlers,
blood donors,
bull riders
briskly
    – some bell bottomed –
went about their business.

Wanting
    – no –
pining warm welcome from others,
their woe buffers worn of scorn's frigid whimsy;
weary of loneliness,
stamina wavering,
    reluctantly,
willpowers waned.

Believers blessedly went about their business
And baptized barbarians went about their business.

Prophetically perhaps, Miss Ma'am once warned,
    "So perfectly wrong and monotone
    be wits of the bleak and blue.
    For wither go whether they body or mind,
    soon go the other'n, too."

        "Maybe."

The bustling, the bereaved went about their business
The birthed, the breathing went about their business.

Possessions none,
disappointments many,
venomous memories,
hopes non-existent,

witnessed by wrath without wisdom's will
were wounded mind and spirit wed.

Then,

Wintry,
wrinkled,
witless,
worthless,
    rightly wardrobed for worlds wile and wilder;
wreaking wisecracks reeking of wretch;
they –
    waiting and
    waiting
just waited.

The breathing,
    unaware of wisdom's rainbow,
happily went about their business.
The breathing,
    knowing little of knowing nothing,
went happily about their business.

* * *

16.
The Sandwich Man

They
     – waiting –
like a beached dinghy
     – sun up –
moored to a barely orange porch
     – sun down –
a porch once so promising,
day after day after time and again,
     bobbing,
     rotting,
     hollow;
baggage crammed with past participles;
ship's log amassed with ill-drawn maps
     – reliable guides to failure;
waiting,
     they
just waiting,
     waited.

Their salt-stained captain
   – determined,
   ever maneuvering,
   always picturing –
believing tracks made for trickery make crossings trying,
   – the corner too, a trap –
twirled obliviously,
rubbed compulsively,
buffed to plasticity
   a platinum sword with powers
while waiting,
   figuring,
garnished impeccably in secondhand tailcoat,
   jelly bean cuff links,
   pale liver tie;
pipe smoking
   – souvenir of optimism –
grumpily chanting cheers
   after tongue-talking grouchisms.

He
   – forever deciphering –
recalculated pranks suffered over,
   over
   and over;
   until,
come a complacent day so complaisant,
as hueless shadows
   – scrutinizing perfunctory devices,
   preparing for preferred vices –
sought guidance from cloud readers recalled as
   "bunch'a witch doctors, Honey; got visions rich and color coded,"
he and amazement,
   – suddenly epiphanized,
   instantly lucid,
   enlightened,
   brilliant –
realized the origin of endless bliss and storm warnings.

Apprising his First Mate of how the unsighted see.
> *"So blind, we've been."*
> *"Miss. Ma'am was right?"*
Once more wanting desperately,
    they awakened hope and need.
News spreading quickly,
cronies joined them,
    choosing to know for themselves.

> *"Only the ones weather the storm gets 'round the corner,"*
silent eyes and a visionless mouth remembered mis-hearing.

Boarding unannounced,
shipmates returning from distant places
had also misheard,
> *"I know stuff bittersweet and drab.*
> *What color stuff y'all know?"*
she asked often.

Hoisting disparagement's anchor, they
casted off wobbling
down the steps swiftly
floating over woodchip ruts,
passed a picket – formerly thistle – fence,
    now sun washed almond-ish, cracked and peeling;
carelessly into chaotic roads rapidly scooting
passed upscalers,
    the faultless,
    the generous when convenient.

They,
a gang of misfits resurrected
    – ignoring swears,
    gestures,
    admonitions;
    their most perfected skill –
glided
    between dreams and hallucinations,

drifted over colorful misadventures,
floated behind trials,
    troubles,
    catastrophes,
cruised around dead end corners,
    over dormant tracks;
with sails steered fiercely by a force unseen:
    the innate want of everyman merely to matter.

They
    – scooting,
    scuttling,
    everybody scurrying –
eventually conquered loafing spots near pawn house windows
peacocked with gadgets
    used,
    blaring,
    giant and tiny,
even antique RCA consoles,
one
    blurry,
    mutilated,
    worthless,
    familiar.

    "For goodness and glory, got'a get 'round the corners,"
Miss. Ma'am told bewilderment often,
    while painting,
    while mending,
    while scrubbing,
    while hoping.

So often the whole mob missed that too,
even more misconstruing,
    "To get my glory, I got a cross ta track,"
stalking blindly a platinum crucifix.

Gripped by insanity's unabridged bile,

a formidable crowd...
   – sweltering, freezing,
   or drenched,
   or parched,
   uncertain which –
without reason heralded,

   "Anyone saying storms into being..."

to cautious passersby,

   "or sunshine"

dramatically flourished for
   travelers unknown,
   travelers unceasing,
   travelers unconcerned,

   "...know who's 'round the corner and
   what's over them tracks! They gon'
   confess today, y'all, for sho'! Ain't they?"

Dutifully, their captain,
scooting on legs wrongly crafted
absolved his repentant crew of blame.
   "So many speak about it,"
was called.
   "But it been so hard to find,"
responded.

Dutifully, their captain,
   priest of perseverance,
   tenacity's paragon scarred by eons of muff,
arose on contorted knees,
removed a brass fedora trimmed with macaroni and cheese.
humbly exposing a head snowcapped and sweating,
as the exulted one,
windmaking sorcerer,
omniscient pansophical prophesier...
   "More!
Astrologer...
   "More!
Storm Speller...

"More!
The weatherman appeared.

Bolstered by eavesdropped snippets from gazers,
  "... I wonder" | "if the sun" | "is shinning?" | "I wonder" |
  "if" | "its raining...This is so" | "exciting." | "I've waited all" |
  "day" | "to know..."
confusion's best battalion
    eager,
    speculating,
    waited until,
following tradition,
before this day's prediction
from a green screen perch,
wisdom spewed.

  "Once we are over the tracks why do we look back?
  As the past stays the same
  so we should accept what we cannot change.
  And for the mistakes who are we to blame
  except our own reflections,
  but we made through
  so we should count our blessings
  instead of second guessing
  history. There is no point in stressing.
  Move forward after learning your lesson(s)."

Everyone, entirely the whole mob,
all enthralled by destiny's messenger,
    missed knowing this message rightly heard,
    wasn't theirs.

United by mis-perception,
    sighing together,
    obeying together,
their quest for value adjourned,
having missed,
  "Today, the son will shine."

A one armed warden in scrubs arrived.

Manners and moods audacious and willful,
    – not knowing their power –
hid like cowards,
      jumping overboard as their wayward vessel
      was loaded into the faded corn
      adorned with all the ones they knew:
      S-A-N-I-T-A-R-I-U-M.

Returned to the place,
    depleted,
    irrelevant,
    non-ratified,
reposing beneath layers of flattery and other earth tones,
they
    – an old man with second-hand sea tales,
    shaded by a rotting canopy,
      maybe crewel,
      maybe worsted;
    and ...
theorizing freestyle,
    ... and ...
re-reorganizing rows of stuffed hares,
        "Rabbits"
    ... and ...
guarding the grave of old trombones
    – a new one,
    unknown,
    needed packing,
    shaping,
    sweeping –
failed to notice nearby sat a single wrinkled hand once grating,
leisurely fanning heat with Someone's obituary;
side-eyeing throngs of gallery patrons across the way.
    So high.
    So mighty.

All consuming ravenously another magnificent opening –
anonymous masterworks titled
"Sandwiches in Oil and Acrylic."

For a synopsis and additional information
or to purchase copies visit

www.arisingtogether.com/sandwichman.html
or
thesandwichmanblog.com

Special thanks to
Dr. Deborah Armintor and Dr. Starita Smith
for unwavering encouragement
given from beginning to end.

Additional appreciation is extended to the following
for helping to make this publication possible:

Prof. Gideon Alorwoyie
Ms. Cheylon Brown
Dr. Brita Coleman
Dr. Karen DeVinney
Dr. Jean Keller

Cover design and illustrations by Donald J. Norman-Cox

www.ingramcontent.com/pod-product-compliance
Lightning Source LLC
Chambersburg PA
CBHW051815040426
42446CB00007B/689